INSECTS DO THE STRANGEST THINGS Of all the worlds of nature there is none so strange as that of the insects. The authors and illustrator of the immensely popular Step-Up Books about the strange doings of animals, birds and fish have joined forces again, and again prove to young readers that fascinating facts can be as much fun as fiction.

INSECTS
do the
STRANGEST
THINGS

by
Leonora and Arthur Hornblow

Illustrations by Michael K. Frith

Step-Up Books — Random House
New York

FOR GWEN HORNBLOW

LEONORA & ARTHUR HORNBLOW are the co-authors of four books in the unique Step-Up nature series: *Animals Do the Strangest Things, Birds Do the Strangest Things, Fish Do the Strangest Things,* and *Insects Do the Strangest Things.*

Arthur Hornblow, Jr. is best known as the movie producer who made such famous films as *Oklahoma, Weekend at the Waldorf, Gaslight* and *Witness for the Prosecution.*

Leonora Hornblow is a columnist, novelist, and author of historical books for children.

The Hornblows live in New York City where they are Associate Members of the American Museum of Natural History and the New York Zoological Society.

MICHAEL K. FRITH is from Bermuda and is a Harvard graduate. At Harvard he co-authored the acclaimed parody thriller *Alligator,* majored in Fine Arts, and was president of the *Harvard Lampoon.* He has since illustrated all four of the Hornblows' books and several books for adults.

Mr. Frith, his wife and two daughters live in New York, where he works as an illustrator, designer and editor of children's books.

This title was originally catalogued by the Library of Congress as follows: Hornblow, Leonora. Insects do the strangest things, by Leonora and Arthur Hornblow. Illus. by Michael K. Frith. New York, Random House [1968] 60 p. col. illus. 21 cm. (Step-up books) Describes nineteen insects that have peculiar and strange characteristics like the camouflage of the walking stick, the driver ants that prefer people to picnics, and the bugs that row themselves like boats on the water's surface. 1. Insects—Juvenile literature. [1. Insects—Habits and behavior] I. Hornblow, Arthur, joint author. II. Frith, Michael K., illus. III. Title. PZ10.H78 In   595.7   68—10046
ISBN: 0-394-80072-9; ISBN: 0-394-90072-3 (lib. bdg.)

Contents

INSECTS DO THE STRANGEST THINGS

The Beautiful Dragon

The dragonfly does not look like a dragon. It does not look like a fly. It looks like a pretty little airplane.

When you see a dragonfly flash by, it probably sees you, too. Its great round eyes are wonderful. It can see everything around it at once.

3

The dragonfly looks more like a dragon when it is young.

The mother dragonfly lays her eggs in the water. The new dragonflies that come out of the eggs are called nymphs. They may be the ugliest and greediest things in the world.

A nymph's long bottom lip has hooks on it. When something swims by, the lip snaps out and hooks it. The nymph gobbles up its victim and looks around for more.

The nymph lives underwater for almost a year. Then, one day, it stops eating. It climbs out of the water. It hangs onto a reed or a twig. It does not move. Its skin splits open. Out comes the dragonfly. Soon it opens its shining wings. It will never close them again.

Twiggy

One of the strangest-looking of all the insects is the walking stick. It looks like a twig. Even its long, thin legs look like twigs. A walking stick sitting on a branch is hard to tell from a real twig. Even hungry birds pass close by without seeing it.

6

The walking stick changes color, too. When it hatches in the spring, it is green like the new leaves. As it grows older it turns brown, the color of the branches where it lives.

When female walking sticks lay their eggs, they just let them drop to the ground. Often many of them lay their eggs at the same time. Some sunny day if you are walking in the woods you may hear a sound like rain. But it is not rain. It is a shower of walking stick eggs.

The Little Workers

Ants are almost everywhere. If you ever go on a picnic, you will see that this is so. You may find a nice place without an ant in sight. You start to eat and soon your food is full of ants. Ick! Where did they all come from?

They were probably living in the ground right under your picnic basket. Many kinds of ants live underground. Their nests are like underground cities. Thousands of ants live together in an ant "city." These ants are called a colony.

Each colony has at least one queen. She is much bigger than the other ants. All she does is lay eggs.

Most of the other ants in the colony are workers. Ant workers never stop working. They build the nest. They keep it clean. They hunt for food. They take care of the queen and the young ants. They feed them and protect them from enemies.

One kind of ant has a very strange way of guarding its nest. These ants live in trees. They use their heads as doors. They let the ants of their own colony in and out. But they will not open the door for ants from any other colony.

But there are some ants that keep other insects in their colonies. These tiny insects are called aphids or "ant cows." Their food is the honeydew they suck from plants. The ants like this sweet juice, too. They "milk" the aphids by rubbing them with their feelers. Out come drops of honeydew. The ants look after "ant cows" as carefully as farmers look after real cows.

There are other kinds of ant
"farmers." These ants cut
pieces out of leaves. They
carry them down to their
underground homes. There
they chew them until they are
soft. Then they spread them
out. In the chewed-up leaves
they plant something called a
fungus. The fungus grows
and the ants eat it. These
ant "farmers" grow their
own food in their under-
ground gardens.

Some ants have an even stranger
way of storing food. An ant has two
stomachs. One is its real stomach.
The other is used to carry food
to the colony. This is for queens,
young ants and the workers who are
too busy to look for food.

The honeypot ants use this other
stomach to store up honeydew. When
they have honeydew left over, they
feed it to young workers. These
young workers get fatter and fatter.
They get so fat they hardly move.
They just hang from the ceiling. If
another ant wants honey, it takes
it from a living honeypot.

The Amazon ant has a strange way
of using other kinds of ants. The
Amazons are fierce fighters. They
fight their way into the nests of
other ants. These ants fight back,
but the Amazons always win. They
grab the young ants. They carry
them back to their own nest. When
the young ants are grown, they
become the Amazons' slaves. They
dig and build for them. They help
them to attack other nests. They
even have to feed them. Without the
slaves the Amazons would die. They
are only good at fighting. They cannot take care of themselves.

The most famous fighters of all the ants are the driver ants of Africa. Most ants live in one place. But the driver ants are almost always on the move. Sometimes millions of driver ants march through the country together. They eat every insect and bird and small animal they can find. They will eat large animals and people who cannot get away. Even elephants run from an army of terrible driver ants.

One thing that driver ants run away from is strong sunshine. It will kill them. That is why they march at night and on gray days.

The marching ants may come to a stream. They cannot swim well. But they can do a very strange thing. Some of them take hold of a root or bush with their strong jaws. Other ants take hold of these ants. Soon there is a "rope" of ants. The water carries it to the other side. Now it is a bridge. The rest of the ants march across it. On they go looking for food.

They will not eat some things other ants love. They do not like sugar or bacon or bread. So if you have a picnic in Africa do not worry about these ants eating your sandwiches. Worry about their eating you.

The Hungry Cloud

Grasshoppers are easy to find. But they are not always easy to catch. They hop fast. And they hop far. They hop right from the time they are born.

Mother grasshoppers make holes in plants or in the ground. There they lay their eggs.

Weeks later, the baby grasshoppers are ready to leave the eggs. One by one, they climb out of the holes and hop away. It is a parade of little grasshoppers.

Soon a baby grasshopper outgrows its skin. The skin splits. The grass-hopper wriggles out. This happens five or six times before the grass-hopper is full grown. Then it has wings and can fly away.

Sometimes a great cloud of grass-hoppers darkens the sky. There may be millions of them. They are called locusts. They land on fields and farms. They eat up every plant and leaf of grass.

In no time there is nothing left
but the bare earth.

In the summer we can often hear
grasshoppers. They make a nice
friendly sound. But hungry grasshoppers are not friends to plants
or people.

Lady Luck

Its real name is the ladybird beetle. But most people call it the ladybug. Many people think it brings good luck. And it does bring good luck to people who grow grapefruit and oranges and lemons. A ladybug is small. But it eats a lot. It eats the aphids and other insects that ruin the fruit trees.

People who live where ladybugs gather are lucky, too. Sometimes thousands and thousands of ladybugs gather in one place. People fill baskets and bottles and bags with them. Then they sell them to fruit growers. The fruit growers turn them loose on the fruit trees.

Ladybugs come to the same gathering places year after year.

You may know the poem, "Ladybug, ladybug, fly away home..." But we really want the ladybugs to stay. The world is lucky to have them.

The Home-Wrecker

Nobody can eat a baseball bat—not a tiger or an ostrich or a man. But the little termite can. Termites eat wood. Soft wood and hard wood, wet wood and dry wood are what they have for breakfast, lunch and dinner.

The wood has to be turned into food to do a termite any good. A termite cannot do this by itself. But it has tiny living things called protozoans inside it. The termite swallows the wood. Then the protozoans turn it into food. Without the protozoans the termite would starve.

Termites often get into houses. This means trouble. They will eat tables and chairs and pianos. They love books, too. The paper is made out of wood.

Most people do not know when there are termites in the house. Termites make no noise. They hide in the wood. They chew away. Sometimes they can chew away a whole house!

But termites are helpful, too. In jungles and forests they eat out the insides of old dead trees. The trees fall down. This makes room for new trees to grow.

Not all termites live in wood. Some of them build amazing houses. Most of these houses are made of dirt. They can be huge. They can be 12 feet thick and 20 feet high. They are very strong, too. Even a man with an axe has a hard time breaking into one.

There are animals like the aardvark who love to eat termites. They are very strong. They have sharp claws for breaking into termites' houses.

Termites are fine insects out of doors. But no one wants them inside. Let them live in their own houses and stay out of ours.

The Green Grabber

The praying mantis sits very still.
It holds up its front legs. It looks
as if it is praying. But the mantis
is not praying. It is waiting. It is
waiting to kill.

There are many sharp spikes on
those long legs. When an insect
comes along, the mantis' legs shoot
out. The spikes dig into the insect.
The mantis bites off its head. Snap!
There goes another insect.

Praying mantises make very good pets. They kill flies and other pests. A mantis will eat right out of your hand. It even seems to like having its back stroked.

Some people tie praying mantises to their beds. The mantis keeps a sharp lookout. It snaps up any insect that comes too close.

So if you ever find a praying mantis take it home with you. It might be the strangest pet you ever had.

27

The Spinaround

In pools and ponds and quiet streams
live little beetles called whirligigs.
They whirl every which way. They
spin like mad across the water.

The whirligig has strange eyes. It
sees above and below the water at
the same time. One half of each eye
looks up. The other half looks down.

Most whirligigs have a bad smell.
This keeps their enemies away. But
one kind smells like fresh apples.
What a strange smell for an insect
to have.

The Runaround

Near the whirligig you may find a little bug called the water strider. Like all insects it has six legs. It holds its short front legs up under its head. It pushes itself along with its long middle legs. And it steers with its back legs. Its body never touches the water. It runs around. It runs so fast it seems to skate on top of the water. Often it jumps into the air. It can land again and not get wet. This is a good thing for the water strider. If it did get wet, it might drown.

The Housebuilder

There is nothing very strange about grown-up caddisflies. But when they are young they do the strangest thing. They build houses and take them wherever they go.

There are many different kinds of caddisfly. Each builds a different kind of house.

A young caddisfly is called a caddis-worm. It hatches underwater. It makes a tube of silky stuff. On this it builds its house. It uses sticks or sand or leaves or little stones.

Some caddisworm houses are round. Some are square. Some look like trumpets. One caddisworm makes a house that looks like a snail shell.

The caddisworm sticks its head and feet out of its front door. Then it walks around with its house right on its back.

One day it closes itself up in its house. It stays there until it is ready to turn into a caddisfly. Then it cuts its way out. It floats to the top of the water. Its skin splits. Out comes the caddisfly. In a flash it flies away.

The Bug Boats

There are two bugs that look like little boats. One is the water boatman. The other is the backswimmer.

The water boatman has long back legs. They look like oars. And it uses them like oars. It rows around on top of the water. Often it rows down to the bottom. There it holds onto a plant with its two middle legs. Its front legs are like spoons. With them it scoops up bits of plants to eat.

A backswimmer looks a lot like a water boatman. But there is an easy way to tell them apart. A water boatman rows along right side up. A backswimmer swims upside down. In winter when a pond freezes, you can see backswimmers walking around upside down under the ice.

Both the backswimmer and the water boatman have wings. If they want to, these little boats can fly. And they both fly right side up.

The Enemies

The housefly and the mosquito are two of man's insect enemies.

Mosquitoes bite. Most mosquito bites just itch. But some can make people very sick.

In some parts of the world there are sicknesses called yellow fever and malaria. These are spread by mosquitoes. A mosquito bites some-one who has malaria. It drinks a little of his blood. Then off it goes and bites someone else. That person catches the malaria. Mosquito bites kill thousands of people every year.

Mosquitoes like to bite at night. That is why in many places beds have nets over them. This keeps the sleeper safe from mosquitoes.

Everyone is safe from the male mosquito. His food is the juice of plants and flowers. It is the female mosquito who likes a bite of you for dinner.

Houseflies cannot bite. But a house-fly is worse than a mosquito. It flies from dirt and garbage right into a house. Its body is covered with germs. So are its sticky feet. Everywhere it goes it leaves germs behind it. A housefly spreads more germs than any mosquito.

Houseflies are pests, too. They buzz around. They land on your nose when you try to sleep. They land on your food when you try to eat.

They bother animals, too. Horses and cows have tails to brush them away. But we need flyswatters and sprays to get rid of them.

Many insects are our friends. But nobody likes a mosquito. And nobody wants a housefly in the house.

The Marvelous Journey

The mother monarch butterfly lays her eggs on a milkweed plant. The eggs are green and very small. They look like drops of dew.

After a few days the eggshell opens. Out comes a tiny dark caterpillar. It begins to eat the milkweed. A strange thing is that it will eat only milk-weed. If it cannot get milk-weed it will starve.

The little caterpillar eats for two weeks. Then comes the time for its wonderful change into a butterfly.

The caterpillar hangs upside down. Its skin splits. It pushes the skin off. Now the caterpillar is a pupa.

The pupa has clear green skin. You can see the butterfly growing inside. In about two weeks the pupa splits. Out crawls the crumpled monarch butterfly.

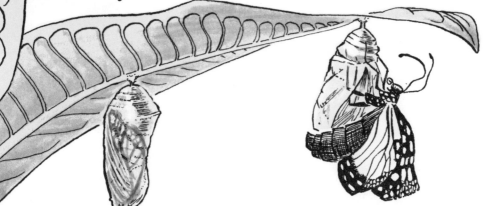

The monarch butterfly spreads its wings for the first time. Slowly it begins to move them. Soon it is strong enough to fly.

For the rest of the summer it flies from flower to flower. Inside the flowers there is a sweet juice called nectar. This is the monarch's food.

Then the days begin to grow cold. Now the monarch is ready to start on a marvelous journey.

Thousands of monarchs begin to fly south together. They fly slowly. They have a long way to go.

Many of the monarchs will die on the journey. Some will be killed by storms. Some will be eaten by birds. Luckily most birds will not eat them. They do not seem to like the way monarchs taste.

At night the monarchs
stop flying. They have
favorite resting places
along the way. Every
year new monarchs
come back to the same
places. Thousands of
bright butterflies cover
the branches of the trees.

Each morning the monarchs
fly on. Their journey may
take five months. They may
fly more than 2,000 miles.

But at last most of them reach the warm, sunny south. They spend the winter there.

In the spring the monarchs start flying back to the north. This time they do not all fly together.

On the way, mother monarchs lay eggs on milkweed plants. Now the monarchs' lives are almost over. One by one, they die. But the eggs hatch. The new monarchs fly on. They fly north, back to where their parents' marvelous journey began.

43

The Silk-Spinner

The silkworm is not a worm at all. It is a caterpillar. If it were left alone, it would turn into a moth. But most silkworms are not left alone.

Billions and billions of silkworms are raised on farms in Japan. Millions and millions of mulberry trees are grown there, too. Mulberry leaves are food for the silkworms.

Silkworms are kept on trays. They are fed fresh mulberry leaves.

After a few weeks, a silkworm stops eating. It raises its head. Out of its mouth comes a very thin thread. It moves its head from side to side. The thread goes round and round its body. In three days the silkworm is closed in a cocoon of thread.

The farmer puts the cocoons in a hot oven or in boiling water. This kills the silkworms inside. Then the cocoons are sent to a silk factory.

At the factory big machines unwind each cocoon. The very thin threads from the cocoons are put together. This makes thicker thread.

Other machines make this thread into beautiful silk cloth.

It takes the thread of about 20,000 cocoons to make just one pound of silk cloth.

Not all cocoons are used to make silk cloth. The farmers let some of the silkworms live. The silkworms turn into moths inside the cocoons. Then they break out.

The moths live only a few days. They do not eat a thing. But each female lays hundreds of little eggs. Most of these hatch into new silkworms. Soon they are at work spinning the silk that makes the most beautiful cloth in the world.

The High Jumper

Grasshoppers are great jumpers. So are frogs and kangaroos. But, for their size, fleas are the best jumpers of them all.

A flea can jump eight inches into the air. This is about a hundred times its height. Think of a man jumping a hundred times his height. He could jump over a building 40 stories high.

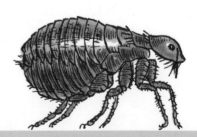

A strange thing about the flea is that it lands looking backward. And its back legs always come down first.

There are people who put on "flea circuses." The fleas do tricks. They jump through hoops. They even pull little carts around. People pay to watch them.

Usually people are not happy to see a flea. Fleas ride on cats and dogs and chickens and mice. They ride on people, too. There is even a kind of flea that lives on snakes. No one wants fleas. Their bites hurt. It is no fun at all to have a flea.

It is very hard to get rid of fleas. They move fast. They are hard and smooth. They slip easily through hair and fur and fingers.

A good way to get rid of fleas is with soap and water. Fleas hate baths. Even the great jumper cannot jump through a soap bubble.

The Honey Factory

For thousands of years men have raised and kept honeybees. Of all the insects, honeybees may be man's best friends.

Bees make wax. Beeswax is used to make floor wax and colored pencils and candles.

Bees help grass and fruit and flowers to grow. There is a yellow powder called pollen in flowers. Bees carry pollen from flower to flower. Plants need this to make new seeds.

If you like honey, thank the honey-bees. Making honey is one of their main jobs. Honey is their main food.

A honeybee's home is called a bee-hive. It can be in a tree or a cave. Or a man may have made it for the bees. There are many rooms in a hive. They are called cells.

Three kinds of bee live in a hive. They are the queen, the drones and the workers. The queen's job is to lay eggs. She can lay 2,000 eggs a day!

From these eggs hatch white grubs.
Some grubs turn into drones. They
are male bees. They do very little.
Most of the grubs become workers.

A worker is wonderfully made for
its life of hard work. The first job
it has is caring for the grubs. Its
body makes a food called royal jelly.
All the grubs are fed royal jelly for
a few days. Then most of them are
fed bee bread. The workers make it
from pollen and honey. These grubs
turn into drones and more workers.

A few grubs are fed only royal jelly.
These grubs become new queens.

When the workers are a little older their bodies start making wax. They use this to make new cells.

Soon they begin their last job. They go out looking for pollen and nectar.

They bring back pollen in "baskets" on their legs. They bring nectar back in their stomachs. In the hive they turn the nectar into honey.

Workers do other things, too. They store the honey and pollen in cells. They take care of the queen. They clean the hive. They keep it cool by fanning their wings. They mend it with sticky stuff called bee glue. And they guard it from enemies.

Every worker bee has a stinger. It will sting anything that tries to take the honey.

The queen does not use her stinger to guard the hive. She uses it only to kill other queens. A hive can have only one queen at a time.

Of all the things the honeybees do, their dance is the strangest. A bee comes back to the hive with nectar and pollen. It begins to dance in circles. The other bees gather to watch. They can tell from the way the bee dances where it found the nectar. They fly right to the same flowers to bring back more.

The way honeybees work together is amazing. They do so many wonderful things. Whoever first made a friend of the busy bee had a good idea.

The Flying Flashlight

On a summer night you may see tiny lights flashing in the dark sky. You may wonder about them. They are fireflies. They are telling each other where they are.

Fireflies are not really flies at all. They are beetles. By day you might not see them. By night they glow. Even their eggs glow. And the grubs that hatch from the eggs glow, too. They are called glowworms.

The strange thing about this light is that it has almost no heat. Man has tried to make light without heat. But he cannot do it.

Some night catch some fireflies. Put them in a glass jar with a top on it. Other fireflies will see their light and come to it. Soon you will have enough light to read this book by.

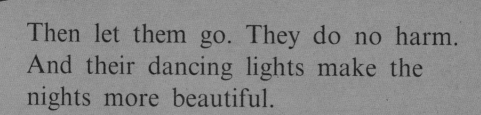

Then let them go. They do no harm. And their dancing lights make the nights more beautiful.

You will find insects almost any-where. Some are our friends. Some are not. But every kind of insect has its place in our strange and wonderful world.